PIANO · VOCAL · GUITAR

THE BEST CONTEMPORARY CHRISTIAN SONGS EVER

ISBN 0-634-01282-7

HAL•LEONARD®
CORPORATION
7777 W. BLUEMOUND RD. P.O. BOX 13819 MILWAUKEE, WI 53213

Visit Hal Leonard Online at
www.halleonard.com

CONTENTS

ABBA
(Father)

Words and Music by REBECCA ST. JAMES,
TEDD TJORNHOM and OTTO PRICE

Moderately fast

I'm __ feel-ing like the ea - gle that ris - es,
Run-ning in this race __ 'til the fin - ish line,

They will soar like ea - gles. ___

ARMS OF LOVE

Words and Music by AMY GRANT,
MICHAEL W. SMITH and GARY CHAPMAN

Slowly, with much expression

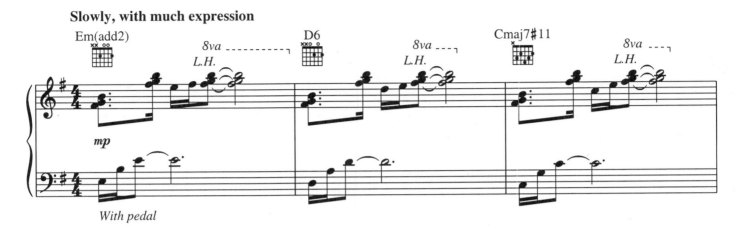

Lord, I'm real - ly glad __ You're here. __

I hope You feel __ the same __ when You __ see all __ my fear, and how I've

AWESOME GOD

Words and Music by
RICH MULLINS

15

THE BASICS OF LIFE

Words and Music by DON KOCH
and MARK HARRIS

We've turned the page, ____ for a new day has dawned, ____ and we've re-ar-ranged ____ what is right and what's wrong, ____

THE COLORING SONG

Words and Music by
DAVE EDEN

Moderately slow, in 2

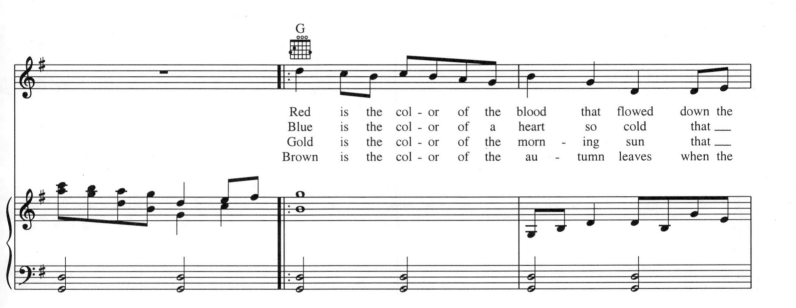

Red is the col-or of the blood that flowed down the
Blue is the col-or of a heart so cold that __
Gold is the col-or of the morn - ing sun that __
Brown is the col-or of the au - tumn leaves when the

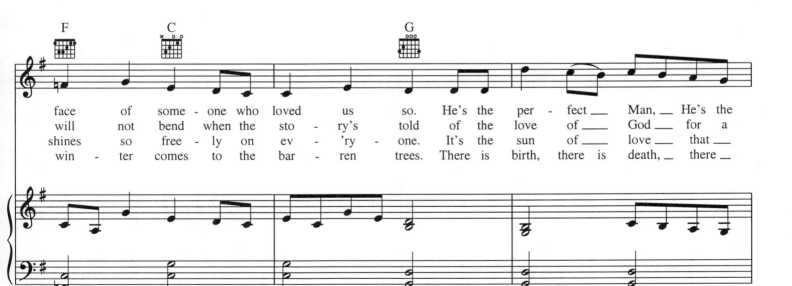

face of some - one who loved us so. He's the per - fect __ Man, __ He's the
will not bend when the sto - ry's told of the love of __ God __ for a
shines so free - ly on ev - 'ry - one. It's the sun of __ love __ that __
win - ter comes to the bar - ren trees. There is birth, there is death, __ there __

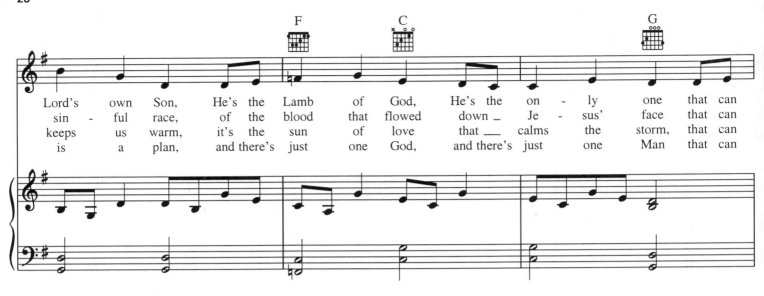

Lord's own Son, He's the Lamb of God, He's the on - ly one that can
sin - ful race, of the blood that flowed down _ Je - sus' face that can
keeps us warm, it's the sun of love that _ calms the storm, that can
is a plan, and there's just one God, and there's just one Man that can

give us life, that can make us grow, that can make the love be -
give us life, that can make us grow, that can keep our hearts from _
give us life, that can make us grow, that can turn our morn - ings _
give us life, that can make us grow, that can make our sins as _

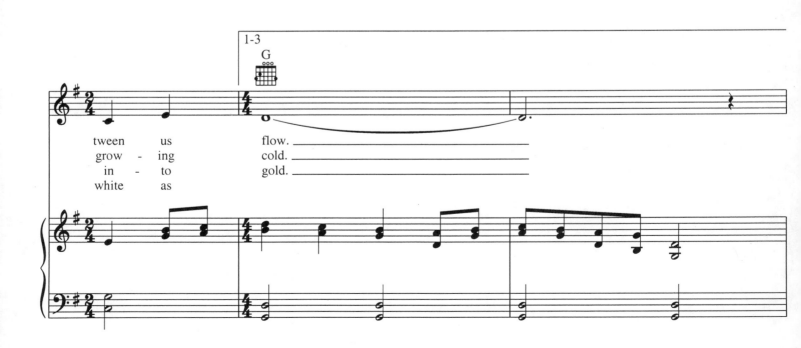

1-3

tween us flow. _____
grow - ing cold. _____
in - to gold. _____
white as

CRUCIFIED WITH CHRIST

Words and Music by RANDY PHILLIPS, DENISE PHILLIPS
DAVE CLARK and DON KOCH

D.S. al Coda

FRIENDS

Words and Music by MICHAEL W. SMITH
and DEBORAH D. SMITH

Moderately slow

Pack-ing up __ the dreams __ God
With the faith __ and love ____ God's

plant-ed
giv-en

in the fer-tile soil __ of __ you,
spring-ing from __ the hope __ we __ know,

can't be-lieve the hopes __ he's grant-ed
we will pray the joy __ you'll live in

means a chap-ter in _____ your life __ is through.
is the strength __ that now __ you show.

EL SHADDAI

Words and Music by MICHAEL CARD
and JOHN THOMPSON

With much expression

El Shad - dai, _____ El Shad - dai, _____ El El - yon _____ na A - do - nai, _____ age to age _____ you're still _____ the same, _____

FATHER'S EYES

Words and Music by
GARY CHAPMAN

Gently

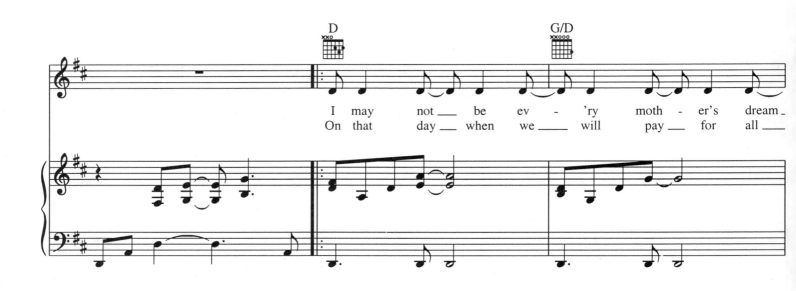

I may not __ be ev - 'ry moth - er's dream __
On that day __ when we __ will pay __ for all __

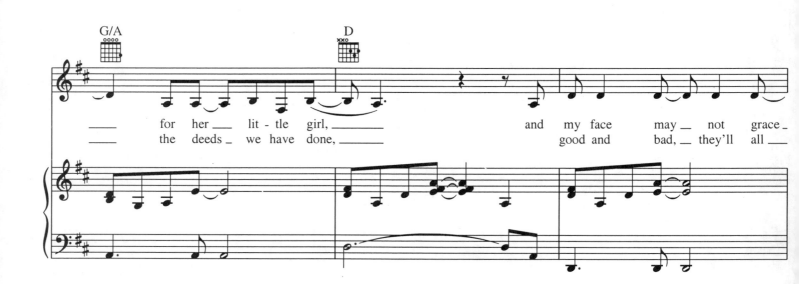

__ for her __ lit - tle girl, __ and my face may __ not grace __
__ the deeds __ we have done, __ good and bad, __ they'll all __

FAVORITE SONG OF ALL

Words and Music by
DAN DEAN

He

loves to hear the wind _ sing as it whis-tles through _ the pines _ on _ moun - tain
loves to hear the an - gels as they sing, _____ "Ho - ly, ho - ly is the

peaks _____
Lamb." _____

and He

when lost sin-ners now _ made clean _

lift their voic - es loud _ and

strong; _____ when those pur - chased by ___ His blood _

lift to Him _ a song _ of love. _

FIND US FAITHFUL

Words and Music by
JON MOHR

pil - grims on __ the jour - ney of the nar - row road, __ and

FRIEND OF A WOUNDED HEART

Words and Music by WAYNE WATSON
and CLAIRE CLONINGER

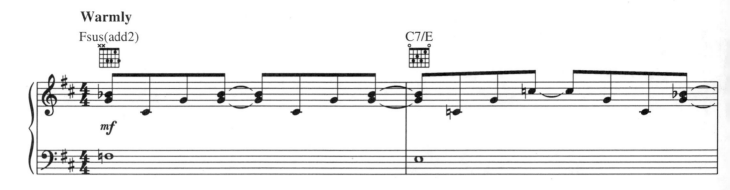

Smile, _____ make 'em _____ think you're _____ hap - py,
Why _____ are the _____ days so _____ lone - ly?
Joy _____ comes _____ like the morn - in';

Repeat ad lib. and Fade

Optional Ending

rit.

GOD IS IN CONTROL

Words and Music by
TWILA PARIS

GOD'S OWN FOOL

Words and Music by
MICHAEL CARD

THE GREAT ADVENTURE

Words and Music by STEVEN CURTIS CHAPMAN
and GEOFF MOORE

Oh, _____ This ___ is The Great Ad-ven-ture. _____

Yeah. _____ Come on _ get read - y, for the ride _____

_____ of your _ life. _____ Gon - na leave _ long - faced _ re - li -

gion _____ in a cloud of dust _ be - hind And dis-cov - er all the new ho - ri -

THE GREAT DIVIDE

Words and Music by MATT HUESMANN
and GRANT CUNNINGHAM

HE WALKED A MILE

Words and Music by
DAN MUCKALA

With much emotion ♩ = 69

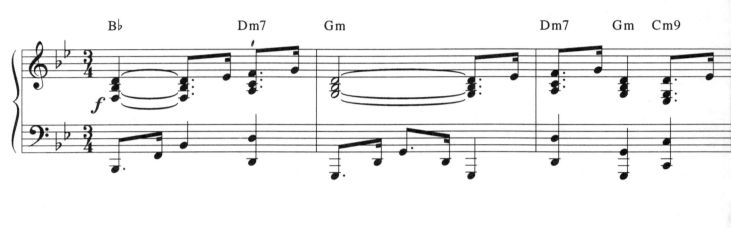

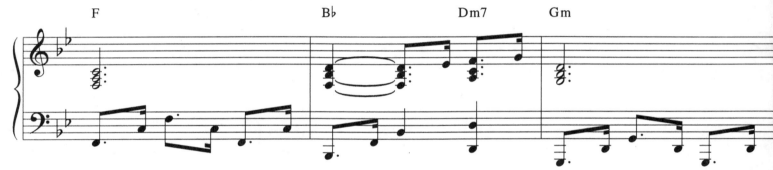

Be -

HEAVEN IN THE REAL WORLD

Words and Music by
STEVEN CURTIS CHAPMAN

I saw it a - gain __
To stand in the pour -

HIS STRENGTH IS PERFECT

Words and Music by STEVEN CURTIS CHAPMAN
and JERRY SALLEY

HIDE MY SOUL

Written by CHRIS EATON
and SHEILA WALSH

Here I am ____ with noth-ing left __ to say; __ how can I e-ven ____ speak? Oh, my dreams __ lie __ scat-tered __ like ash - es be - neath my ____ feet. Can you see

nothing I __ can do, __ nothing that I __ can say. __

You a - lone __

____ are the an - chor of __ my soul; don't let it slip a - way. __

Fm9

And You see _____ all the pain be - hind __ my smile, ____ the

(Ah. _____)

Bb(add2)

tears run down __ my face. _____ Will the sun ___ ev - er shine __

D.S. al Coda

HOW BEAUTIFUL

Words and Music by
TWILA PARIS

I MISS THE WAY

Words and Music by MICHAEL W. SMITH
and WAYNE KIRKPATRICK

Once a true _____ be-liev - er,
Now you move _ in oth - er cir - cles,
Some are call - ing you _ a prod - i - gal,

once there was _ a fi - re in _ your _ soul.
to the beat _ of dif - f'rent _ drums,
and some aren't call - ing you _ at _ all. and

You were the _ e - pit - o - me _ of bless - ed faith _ a - stir, with thirst for ho -
I see on - ly glimps - es of _ the one _ you used _ to be, the in - spir -
But far a - way _ some - one _ is call - ing you _ back home, but do you hear _

I'LL LEAD YOU HOME

Words and Music by MICHAEL W. SMITH
and WAYNE KIRKPATRICK

IF YOU COULD SEE ME NOW

Words and Music by
KIM NOBLITT

Very slowly and freely

Our

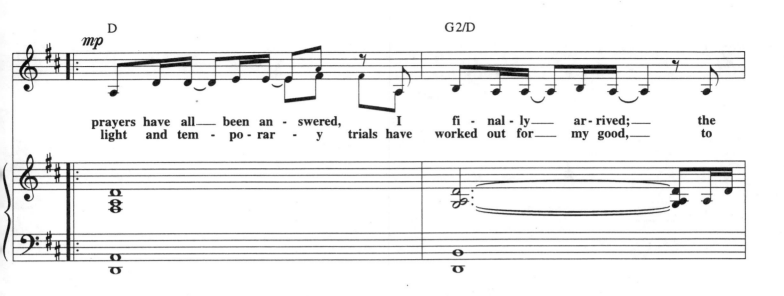

prayers have all— been an-swered, I fi-nal-ly— ar-rived;— the
light and tem-po-rar-y trials have worked out for— my good,— to

heal-ing that— had been— de-layed— has now been re-al-ized.—
know it brought— Him glo-ry— when I mis-un-der-stood.—

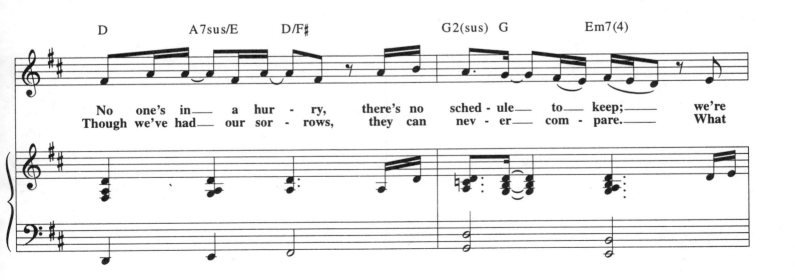

No one's in a hur-ry, there's no sched-ule— to— keep;— we're
Though we've had— our sor-rows, they can nev-er— com-pare.— What

N.C.

very slowly and freely

p

—— me now,

if you could on - ly

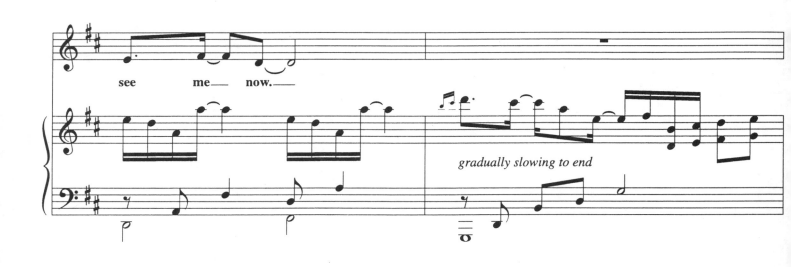

see me now.——

gradually slowing to end

p

p

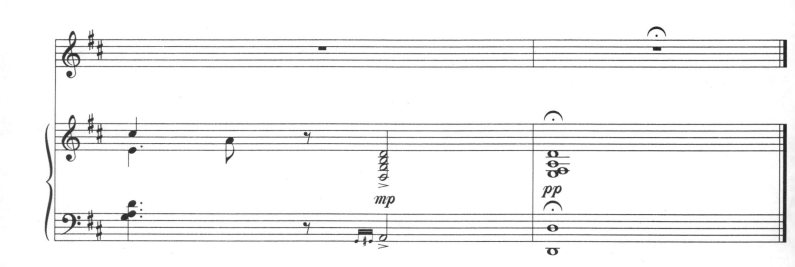

mp

pp

IN A DIFFERENT LIGHT

Words and Music by JODY McBRAYER, CHERIE PALIOTTA,
MICHAEL PASSONS, JANNA POTTER and MATT HUESMANN

Don't cry for me. ___
Don't be a - fraid ___

No, I've ___ nev - er been ___ one to shoul - der the weight ___ of the world. ___
of the twists ___ and the turns ___ of the road ___ that we're on. ___ Just be - lieve ___

IN THE NAME OF THE LORD

Words by GLORIA GAITHER, PHILL McHUGH and SANDI PATTY
Music by SANDI PATTY

JESUS FREAK

Words and Music by TOBY McKEEHAN
and MARK HEIMERMANN

Peo-ple say I'm strange, does it ___ make me a strang - er that my best friend was born ___

___ in a man - ger?

___ in a man - ger? ___

JESUS WILL STILL BE THERE

Words and Music by JOHN MANDEVILLE
and ROBERT STERLING

JOY IN THE JOURNEY

Words and Music by
MICHAEL CARD

1., 3. There is a joy____ in____ the jour - ney,
all who've been born____ of____ the Spir - it

there's a light____
and who____

JUST ONE

Words and Music by CONNIE HARRINGTON
and JIM COOPER

Free-Spirited Rock

mf

As we change

(Harmony 2nd time only)

as a man, _____ and the an- swers are a dime a doz-
much at stake _____ to be wast- ing time on im- i- ta-

- en, points of view _____ are like sand _____ stretch-in' out
- tions, prom- i- ses _____ (prom- i- ses) and ___ claims. _____ There will nev-

LEAN ON ME

Words and Music by
KIRK FRANKLIN

Moderately, with emotion

Spoken: This is for that little child with no father, for that man that doesn't have a place to stay, and for that little boy living with AIDS— you can lean on me.

LET US PRAY

Words and Music by
STEVEN CURTIS CHAPMAN

I hear you say __ your heart __ is ach - ing, you've got trou - ble in the mak-
So when we feel __ the Spir - it mov - ing, prompt-ing, prod-ding and be-hoov-

- ing, and you ask __ if I'll __ be pray-ing for __ you, please. __
- ing, there is no __ time to be los - ing, let us pray. __

THE LION AND THE LAMB

By ANNE BARBOUR and
BILL BATSTONE

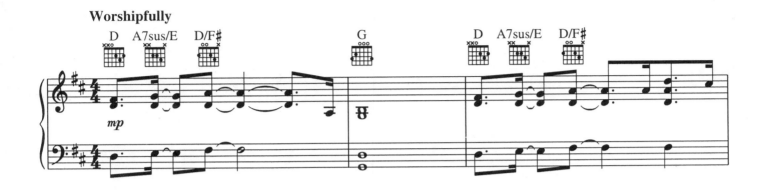

Who is __ He __ who's the might - i - est __ of all?

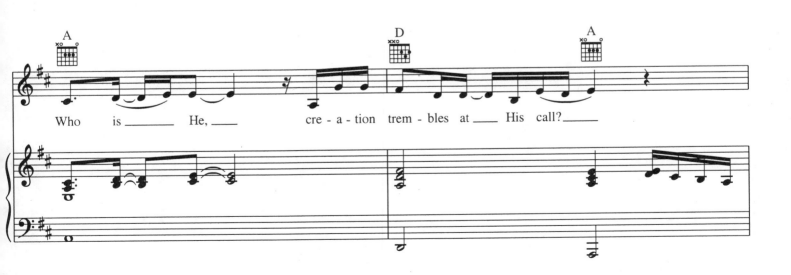

Who is ___ He, ___ cre - a - tion trem - bles at __ His call? ___

LOVE IN ANY LANGUAGE

Words and Music by JOHN MAYS
and JON MOHR

Moderately slow, in 2

*Je-

t'aime,   **Te   a   -   mo,   ***Ya - tyi - bya   lyu
teach the young _ our dif - f'ren - ces,   yet   look   how we're   the

blyu,   ****A - ni _____ o - he - vet oth - ka, _____
same;   We   love   to laugh, _ we dream _____ our   dreams, _

* French   *** Russian (phonetic)
** Spanish   **** Hebrew

LOVE WILL BE OUR HOME

Words and Music by
STEVEN CURTIS CHAPMAN

THE MISSION

Words and Music by RANDALL DENNIS
and JON MOHR

1. There's a call go-ing out a-cross the land___ in ev-'ry na-

2. Let us then___ be so-ber, mov-ing on-ly in___ the Spir-

or a-round the world, the mis-sion's still the same:_ pro-claim and live_ the truth_ in Je - sus' name!_

2nd time to CODA

sub. _mp_

_mp_

28

3. As a can-dle is_ con-sumed_ by the pas - sion of_ the flame,_

CODA

To love the Lord___ our God___ is the heart-
- beat of___ our mis-sion, the spring from which___ our ser-vice o-ver-flows..
___ A-cross the street___ or a-round the world,___ the
mis-sion's still the same:___ pro-claim and live___ the truth___ in Je-sus' To
name!___

MY UTMOST FOR HIS HIGHEST

Words and Music by
TWILA PARIS

With conviction ♩ = 80

1. When the Sav - ior came to earth, an - swer to the end - less fall, He be - came a man by
2. Stand - ing in this ho - ly place, let us all re - mem - ber here, cov - ered on - ly by His

OH LORD, YOU'RE BEAUTIFUL

Words and Music by
KEITH GREEN

ON MY KNEES

Words and Music by DAVID MULLEN,
NICOLE COLEMAN-MULLEN and MICHAEL HUNTER OCHS

1. There are days___ when I feel___ the best of me___ is

2. I can be___ in a crowd___ or by my-self,___ is

read - y to_____ be - gin._____ Then there're days_____
al - most an - y - where,_____ when I feel_____

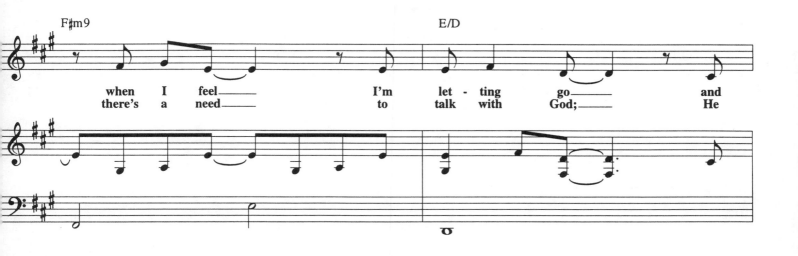

when I feel_____ I'm let - ting go_____ and
there's a need_____ to talk with God;_____ He

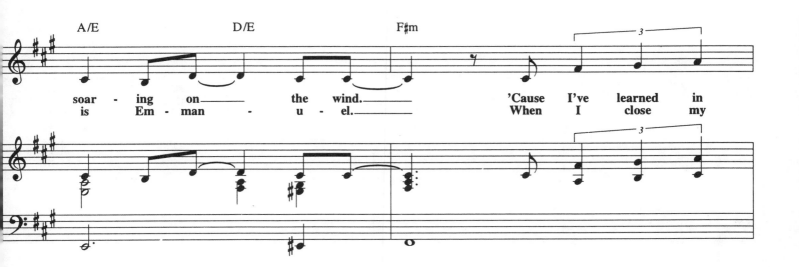

soar - ing on_____ the wind._____ 'Cause I've learned in
is Em - man - u - el._____ When I close my

PEOPLE NEED THE LORD

Words and Music by PHILL McHUGH
and GREG NELSON

Ev - 'ry day they pass me by. I can see it
We are called they to take His light to a world where

in their eye; Emp - ty peo - ple filled with care,
wrong seems right; What could be too great a cost for

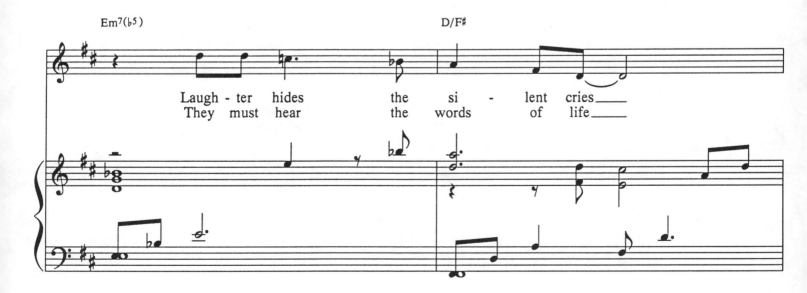

PLACE IN THIS WORLD

Words by WAYNE KIRKPATRICK and AMY GRANT
Music by MICHAEL W. SMITH

The wind _ is mov - ing, _ but I _ am stand - ing still. _
If there _ are mil - lions, _ down _ on _ their knees, _

A life _ of _ pag - es _ wait - ing to _ be _ filled.
a - mong _ the man - y _ can You still _ hear _ me?

270

STILL CALLED TODAY

Words and Music by
STEVEN CURTIS CHAPMAN

SERVE THE LORD

Words and Music by
CARMAN

By the grace of God __ I will serve ____ the Lord. __

By the grace of God __

I will serve the Lord.

rit.

a tempo

rit.

THANK YOU

Words and Music by
RAY BOLTZ

THY WORD

Words and Music by
MICHAEL W. SMITH and AMY GRANT

Thy Word is a lamp un-to my feet and a light un-to my path.

Thy Word is a lamp un-to my feet and a

VIA DOLOROSA

Words and Music by BILLY SPRAGUE
and NILES BOROP

WE CAN MAKE A DIFFERENCE

Words and Music by MARK HEIMERMANN
and DAVID MULLEN

We live in a—— dream—— if we real - ly think——
Do you know a—— man—— who's need - ing a hand?——

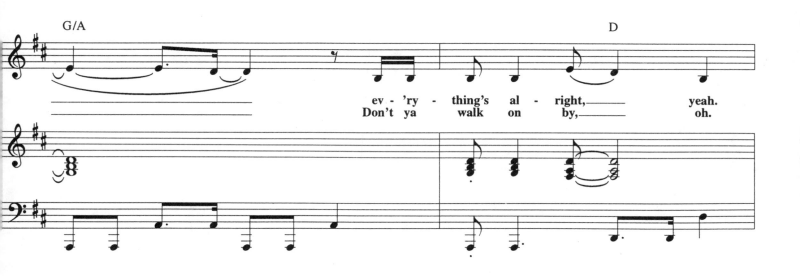

ev - 'ry - thing's al - right,——— yeah.
Don't ya walk on by,——— oh.

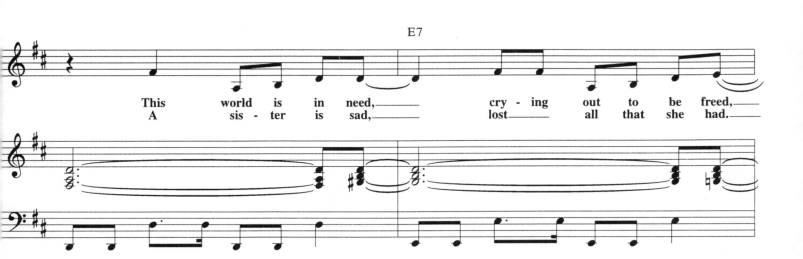

This world is in need,—— cry - ing out to be freed,——
A sis - ter is sad,—— lost—— all that she had.——

we got - ta shed some light,_____ oh.
We got - ta take the time,_____ oh.

Teach the world to smile_____ and hear an - gels sing;_____
Look a - round your world,_____ it will test - i - fy._____

feel the breath of God_____ and the pow'r__ it brings.
Some have emp - ty hearts,_____ some have hun - gry eyes._____

WHEN GOD'S PEOPLE PRAY

Words and Music by
WAYNE WATSON

With conviction ♩ = 104

Trou - ble knock - ing on your
Hope - less sit - u - a - tion

win - dow pane,_____ storm - y weath - er at your_____ door,_____
turns a - round,_____ di - lem - ma pass - es by and_____ by.

peo - ple pray.

Oh,___ when God's peo - ple pray.___

When God's peo - ple

pray.___

WHERE THERE IS FAITH

Words and Music by
BILLY SIMON

THE WARRIOR IS A CHILD

Words and Music by
TWILA PARIS

336